Welcome To The RISE Of The New Temple Of God Memory Book

I0272842

Written By
Sister Kadee

Sister Kadee

About The Author:

Sister Kadee was raised from the dead at the age of 15 by Jesus on Christmas Day, 1993 after being hospitalized with bacterial spinal meningitis. Doctors flooded her body with IV fluids failing her kidneys, filling her lungs, and her ankles swelled to the size of watermelons as she was rolled into an isolation room to die with no visitors allowed.

Her grandfather, forcing his way in to lay hands on her and give her a blessing, raised her up. Her passion to serve the Lord has been met with disdain by every church she has ever attended. Kadee has helped 1000's of people to accept Jesus as their Savior who feel out of place at church. This very special Memory Book was first compiled by a Bible

reading radical preacher who spearheaded the Jesus Revolution of the 1970's, USA.

Sister Kadee's first mission using the Memory Book as a tool.

C. Rose, 1997

"I felt like a prisoner in an assisted living facility, and I was only 18. I was afraid of everyone and everything for as long as I could remember. Diagnosed with several mental conditions including PTSD and Agoraphobia due to the traumatic abuse of being sold to truck drivers by my step dad from the age of 8 - 13. I was taking several medications. I had been seen by top mental health professionals and admitted to inpatient care several times.

After just 3 weeks working with Sister Kadee, receiving Jesus as my personal savior and memorizing just a few of the verses in this memory book, my life was transformed drastically. My case was closed as a miracle, and after my Discipleship course with her I went to India to work with the deaf as a missionary. I am nearly deaf myself from the abuse I suffered as a child, and she helped me turn my curse into a blessing to help others".

"After this experience with C. Rose, I knew it was my life's purpose to be a minister and healer outside of the confines of modern medicine and religion. I had seen the power of God THROUGH me to help someone else, and there was no going back. The building blocks within these pages will help establish yourself as a living stone, a Living Temple built upon the Chief Corner Stone whom the builders refused as their Messiah".

~*Sister Kadee*

Introduction

And what agreement has the Temple of God with idols? For YOU are the Temple of the living God as God has said, I will dwell in them, and walk in them; and I will be their God, and they shall be my people.

2 Corinthians 6:16

Thy Word have I hid in my heart, That I might not sin against Thee.

Psalsm 119:11

As Man thinks in his heart, so is he.

Proverbs 23:7

He sent His Word and delivered them, and healed them from their destructions. Psalm 107:20

God is a Spirit, and they that worship Him must worship Him in Spirit and in Truth. John 4:24

Memorizing God's word is so important as no one will ever be able to take it from you. Spending time to understand the Bible is foundational to building a relationship with God, as it is His story, like a love letter to His children He is trying to guide back home.

Sister Kadee

In this age of Deception we cannot just believe what people say, especially others who use scripture to justify evil, idolatry, sin, and wickedness. The Devil himself knows the Bible very well, probably better than most Christians. He used scripture to tempt Jesus to stray from His Father's will and is notorious for doing the same today, even from within the church. What was Jesus's response when rebuking the accuser and his temptations? He quoted the written Word of God He had memorized from reading from the Prophets! He didn't make anything up or create a new way to defeat the temptations and deception of Satan.

If WE don't study and memorize scriptures, hiding them in our heart and letting them guide our lives we miss out on the fullness of our potential in this world as Sons and Daughters of the Most High God!

"If you are a Believer of Christ who feels out of place…. You're in the right place."

Sister Kadee

Memorization Tips

1. Write the verse you are working on down on a 3x5 card, piece of paper or small notebook to carry with you throughout the day.

2. Read it outloud, several times, several times each day.

3. Read the verse reference before and after each verse.

4. Record yourself reading and play it several times a day.

5. Review each section for several days before checking the boxes and moving on to the next.

6. Tell others what you are learning and doing! Find an accountability partner to practice with.

Table of Contents

SALVATION 1
    Commentary 4
HOLY SPIRIT 6
    Commentary 7
DISCIPLESHIP 9
    Commentary 12
RELATIONSHIP TO THE WORLD 14
    Commentary 15
PARENTS/FAMILY WORLDLY 17
    Commentary 18
BACKSLIDERS 19
    Commentary 20
OUR JOB 22
    Commentary 25
THE WORD 28
    Commentary 30
LOVE 32
    Commentary 35

IT'S ONLY JESUS	38
Commentary	39
FAITH	42
Commentary	45
PRAYER	47
Commentary	50
HEALING	52
Commentary	55
FREEDOM FROM FEAR	57
Commentary	60
OVERCOMING THE ENEMY	62
Commentary	64
TRIALS AND TESTS	66
Commentary	69
CHASTENING	71
Commentary	72
PERSECUTION	73
Commentary	75
THANKFULNESS & COMPLAINING	76
Commentary	77

FAITHFULNESS & OBEDIENCE	79
Commentary	80
YIELDEDNESS	82
Commentary	83
LEADERS	85
Commentary	86
FRUITFULNESS	88
Commentary	89
GIVING	90
Commentary	91
SUPPLY	93
Commentary	95
END OF THE WORLD	97
Commentary	102
DAY OF THE LORD	105
Commentary	107
SATAN LOOSED	110
Commentary	110
FINAL JUDGMENT	113
Commentary	114

NEW HEAVEN & EARTH	115
Commentary	116
FLAT EARTH	118
Commentary	121
CONCLUSIONS	125

Sister Kadee

SALVATION

John 3:16-17

For God so loved the world, that he gave his only begotten Son, that whosoever believeth in him should not perish, but have everlasting life. For God sent not his Son into the world to condemn the world; but that the world through him might be saved.

John 14:6

Jesus saith unto him, I am the way, the truth, and the life: no man cometh unto the Father, but by me.

Acts 4:12

Neither is there salvation in any other: for there is none other name under heaven given among men, whereby we must be saved.

John 3:3

Jesus answered and said unto him, Verily, verily, I say unto thee, Except a man be born again, he cannot see the kingdom of God.

Matthew 18:3

And said, Verily I say unto you, Except ye be converted, and become as little children, ye shall not enter into the kingdom of heaven.

John 1:12

But as many as received him, to them gave he power to become the sons of God, even to them that believe on his name.

Revelation 3:20

Behold, I stand at the door, and knock: if any man hear my voice, and open the door, I will come in to him, and will sup with him, and he with me.

Romans 3:23

For all have sinned, and come short of the glory of God;

Romans 6:23

For the wages of sin is death; but the gift of God is eternal life through Jesus Christ our Lord. 8

1 John 1:9

If we confess our sins, he is faithful and just to forgive us our sins, and to cleanse us from all unrighteousness.

Romans 10:9-10,13

That if thou shalt confess with thy mouth the Lord Jesus, and shalt believe in thine heart that God hath raised him from the dead, thou shalt be saved. For with the heart man believeth unto righteousness; and with the mouth confession is made unto salvation. For whosoever shall call upon the name of the Lord shall be saved.

Ephesians 2:8-9

For by grace are ye saved through faith; and that not of yourselves: it is the gift of God: Not of works, lest any man should boast.

Titus 3:5

Not by works of righteousness which we have done, but according to his mercy he saved us, by the washing of regeneration, and renewing of the Holy Ghost;

Acts 16:31

And they said, Believe on the Lord Jesus Christ, and thou shalt be saved, and thy house.

John 3:36

He that believeth on the Son hath everlasting life: and he that believeth not the Son shall not see life; but the wrath of God abideth on him.

John 10:28

And I give unto them eternal life; and they shall never perish, neither shall any man pluck them out of my hand.

2 Corinthians 5:17

Therefore if any man be in Christ, he is a new creature: old things are passed away; behold, all things are become new.

Commentary

- Salvation is simple!--All you have to do is receive Jesus, God's Son, as your Savior by asking Him into your heart.

- God loved YOU so much that He gave Jesus to die for your sins, to take your punishment for you.

- The most important will of God for you is that you recognise Jesus as the Son of God believe, on Him as your Saviour and receive His Love.

- God will forgive you for every sin in the book, except one, and that is rejecting Jesus.

- We receive salvation as a pure gift, not because we're good enough or because we deserve it or earn it, but because He loves us and He gives it.

- Grace + Faith + Nothing!--That's salvation.

- Jesus will not force Himself on you, but He waits lovingly and meekly for you to invite Him in. 9

- Don't try to figure Him out--just let Him in.

- Once you have received Jesus, you cannot lose Him! Once saved, always saved.

- True salvation is by pure faith in God's Word, not faith in feelings.

- When you receive Jesus, your whole life is changed, like a newborn baby born into a whole new world with a new spirit as a new child of God! The LIGHT of the world.

HOLY SPIRIT

Acts 1:8

But ye shall receive power, after that the Holy Ghost is come upon you: and ye shall be witnesses unto me both in Jerusalem, and in all Judaea, and in Samaria, and unto the uttermost part of the earth.

John 7:38

He that believeth on me, as the scripture hath said, out of his belly shall flow rivers of living water.

Luke 11:13

If ye then, being evil, know how to give good gifts unto your children: how much more shall your heavenly Father give the Holy Spirit to them that ask him?

John 14:26

But the Comforter, which is the Holy Ghost, whom the Father will send in my name, he shall teach you all things, and bring all things to your remembrance, whatsoever I have said unto you.

John 15:26

But when the Comforter is come, whom I will send unto you from the Father, even the Spirit of truth, which proceedeth from the Father, he shall testify of me:

Galatians 5:22-23

But the fruit of the Spirit is love, joy, peace, longsuffering, gentleness, goodness, faith, Meekness, temperance: against such there is no law.

Acts 2:17

And it shall come to pass in the last days, saith God, I will pour out of my Spirit upon all flesh: and your sons and your daughters shall prophesy, and your young men shall see visions, and your old men shall dream dreams:

Commentary

- The primary purpose of the power of the Holy Spirit is to help you to be a witness! To fill you with such power that you will blast off of your launch pad "into all the world, preaching the Gospel to every creature". (Mark 16:15)

- To be "baptised" in the Holy Spirit means to be completely immersed, filled with and overflowing the Spirit of God. Like pouring water into a glass until it's filled up and running over.

- The baptism of the Holy Spirit is an overflowing baptism of Love. Love for God, Love for yourself, and Love for the lost. Love enough to witness and win others to the Lord's Kingdom.

- If you are going to be a good witness, a real soul-winner, the Holy Ghost is essential!

- The Holy Spirit is like a loving Mother, always gently loving, wooing, comforting, winning, soothing and healing--just like a good mother.

- The Holy Spirit is a sample here and now of what we are going to receive in the afterlife, in Heaven.

- When you ask God for the Holy Ghost, you'll know you've received it because you believe the Bible, which says "Ask and ye shall receive." (Luke 11:9-13)

- Receiving the wonderful Spirit of God is almost like a sexual orgasm! You explode with the Love of God and want to tell everyone about Jesus.

DISCIPLESHIP

Luke 14:33

So likewise, whosoever he be of you that forsaketh not all that he hath, he cannot be my disciple.

Matthew 19:29

And every one that hath forsaken houses, or brethren, or sisters, or father, or mother, or wife, or children, or lands, for my name's sake, shall receive an hundredfold, and shall inherit everlasting life.

Luke 9:23-24

And he said to them all, If any man will come after me, let him deny himself, and take up his cross daily, and follow me. For whosoever will save his life shall lose it: but whosoever will lose his life for my sake, the same shall save it.

Matthew 9:37-38

Then saith he unto his disciples, The harvest truly is plenteous, but the labourers are few; Pray ye therefore the Lord of the harvest, that he will send forth labourers into his harvest.

Matthew 22:14

For many are called, but few are chosen.

Matthew 6:24

No man can serve two masters: for either he will hate the one, and love the other; or else he will hold to the one, and despise the other. Ye cannot serve God and mammon.

Acts 2:44-45

And all that believed were together, and had all things common; And sold their possessions and goods, and parted them to all men, as every man had need.

John 13:35

By this shall all men know that ye are my disciples, if ye have love one to another.

John 8:31-32

Then said Jesus to those Jews which believed on him, If ye continue in my word, then are ye my disciples indeed; And ye shall know the truth, and the truth shall make you free.

John 15:8

Herein is my Father glorified, that ye bear much fruit; so shall ye be my disciples.

Sister Kadee

John 15:16

Ye have not chosen me, but I have chosen you, and ordained you, that ye should go and bring forth fruit, and that your fruit should remain: that whatsoever ye shall ask of the Father in my name, he may give it you.

1 Corinthians 6:19-20

What? know ye not that your body is the temple of the Holy Ghost which is in you, which ye have of God, and ye are not your own? For ye are bought with a price: therefore glorify God in your body, and in your spirit, which are God's.

Commentary

• A disciple is one who follows the teachings of Jesus Christ.

• A disciple forsakes everything, walks with Jesus, follows Jesus and lives with Jesus. This is the difference between mere Christians and Disciples.

• You will never know the fullness of the joy of serving God to the utmost until you have forsakenall to follow Jesus Christ.

• If God is worth serving at all, He's worth serving full time and all the way!

• If the Devil can't keep you from being a pew Christian, he'll do all in his power to keep you from being a revolutionary disciple!

• Time and time again, Jesus' acid test for His prospective disciples was if they were willing to forsake all, drop everything, leave it ALL behind and follow Him.

• This is always the greatest witness to others: When you really give up everything and forsake all to follow Jesus and devote your full time in service to Him.

• Jesus bought and paid for us, we are His property. We belong to Him now! You don't just belong to yourself anymore and you can't just do as you please.

- You either work for God, or you are going to have to work for the Devil. One or the other, the choice is yours.

- If you want to follow Jesus 100% you have got to forsake all and preach the Gospel.

- If you choose God's way, when you see Jesus and the results you're going to know it was worth it all!

- Giving your life to His service in an eternal investment that will pay dividends in Heaven, and souls forever and ever and ever.

- Watch and pray, that you enter not into temptation that might lead you astray from the straight and narrow way which leads to the highest crown and greatest reward. (Mat. 26:41; 7:13,14; Phil. 3:13,14)

- Only one life, 'twill soon be past. Only what's done for Christ will last! What are you doing? For whom? Will it last forever for Jesus and others?

- He is no fool who gives what he cannot keep to gain that which he cannot lose!

- It is better to die for something that to live, and die for nothing. Start living TODAY! There is only ONE WAY! FOR JESUS!!!

RELATIONSHIP TO THE WORLD

James 4:4

Ye adulterers and adulteresses, know ye not that the friendship of the world is enmity with God? whosoever therefore will be a friend of the world is the enemy of God.

John 15:19

If ye were of the world, the world would love his own: but because ye are not of the world, but I have chosen you out of the world, therefore the world hateth you.

2 Timothy 2:4

No man that warreth entangleth himself with the affairs of this life; that he may please him who hath chosen him to be a soldier.

1 John 2:15-17

Love not the world, neither the things that are in the world. If any man love the world, the love of the Father is not in him. For all that is in the world, the lust of the flesh, and the lust of the eyes, and the pride of life, is not of the Father, but is of the world. And the world passeth away, and the lust thereof: but he that doeth the will of God abideth for ever.

2 Corinthians 6:14

Be ye not unequally yoked together with unbelievers: for what fellowship hath righteousness with unrighteousness? and what communion hath light with darkness?

2 Corinthians 6:17

Wherefore come out from among them, and be ye separate, saith the Lord, and touch not the unclean thing; and I will receive you.

Ephesians 5:11

And have no fellowship with the unfruitful works of darkness, but rather reprove them.

Romans 12:2

And be not conformed to this world: but be ye transformed by the renewing of your mind, that ye may prove what is that good, and acceptable, and perfect, will of God.

Commentary

- We are a mighty army of Christian soldiers fighting a relentless war for the TRUTH and LOVE of God against the System's Godless Schools, Christless churches and heartless Mammon.

- Why is God so against this World and its systems? Because they are against Him! In fact, not only are "they" against HIm, but they are of the Devil!

- Materialism is the major religion of the world, and although most people worship the things they can see, there are actually wicked spiritual forces behind this idolatry that they can't see! (Luke 4:5-8)

- The system is your servant, because it is God's servant and serves His purposes. Let it serve yours. Use it But watch out, don't let it use you.

- Whatever this world has to offer, it's only for a little while. But service for the Lord is forever!

PARENTS/FAMILY WORLDLY

Psalms 27:10

When my father and my mother forsake me, then the Lord will take me up.

Matthew 10:36-38

And a man's foes shall be they of his own household. He that loveth father or mother more than me is not worthy of me: and he that loveth son or daughter more than me is not worthy of me. And he that taketh not his cross, and followeth after me, is not worthy of me.

Mark 3:33,35

And he answered them, saying, Who is my mother, or my brethren? For whosoever shall do the will of God, the same is my brother, and my sister, and mother.

Mark 6:4

But Jesus said unto them, A prophet is not without honour, but in his own country, and among his own kin, and in his own house.

Commentary

- One of the first tests for newly called disciples is often the opposition of family and friends. God allows this to see if you love Him enough to put HIM first by forsaking all immediately to follow Him now!

- The father of James and John who stuck by the business, and the rest of their family vanished into obscurity and oblivion, whereas those smelly dirty fisherman sons of his wandered off with a perfect Stranger and made history that has helped save millions of souls for eternity.

- The Scripture says to "obey our parents in the Lord". (Ephesians 6:1-2). If your flesh parents don't love Jesus and aren't preaching the Gospel full-time, they are not your parents in the Lord, and you should obey those who have given birth to you spiritually and who care for your spiritual welfare.

BACKSLIDERS

Luke 9:62

And Jesus said unto him, No man, having put his hand to the plough, and looking back, is fit for the kingdom of God.

Mark 8:36-38

For what shall it profit a man, if he shall gain the whole world, and lose his own soul? Or what shall a man give in exchange for his soul? Whosoever therefore shall be ashamed of me and of my words in this adulterous and sinful generation; of him also shall the Son of man be ashamed, when he cometh in the glory of his Father with the holy angels.

Luke 17:32

Remember Lot's wife.

2 Peter 2:20

For if after they have escaped the pollutions of the world through the knowledge of the Lord and Saviour Jesus Christ, they are again entangled therein, and overcome, the latter end is worse with them than the beginning.

Ezra 8:22b

The hand of our God is upon all them for good that seek him; but his power and his wrath is against all them that forsake him.

Galatians 5:1

Stand fast therefore in the liberty wherewith Christ hath made us free, and be not entangled again with the yoke of bondage.

Revelation 3:11

Behold, I come quickly: hold that fast which thou hast, that no man take thy crown.

Hebrews 11:15-16

And truly, if they had been mindful of that country from whence they came out, they might have had opportunity to have returned. But now they desire a better country, that is, an heavenly: wherefore God is not ashamed to be called their God: for he hath prepared for them a city.

Commentary

- You are either growing and progressing or you are backsliding, one or the other. You cannot stand still.

- Once God has spoken to you and called you, God will never let you be happy or satisfied doing anything else but what He wants you to do.

- When you start failing God, backsliding and going against the Lord, everything goes wrong, supply and provisions fail, health and vitality is lost, and you just spin your wheels.

- Backsliders forsake all too! They forsake the Word, the Lord, the Life, the Light, and the vision of eternity.

- Unrepentant backsliders will enter into Heaven with shame and contempt with no reward because they failed God, they disobeyed, backslid, rebelled against His will, and failed to get the job done. (Daniel 12:2)

- No matter how far you backslide or how far you try to get away from the Lord, you will never be able to escape Him. The "Hound of Heaven" will track you down no matter where you are!

- If you will even start going God's way, if you turn toward Him and try to find your way Home, the Father will come running toward you and take you into His arms!

- Are you living in the Word and Work and Love of the Lord so deep that you could never think of leaving?

OUR JOB

Mark 16:15

And he said unto them, Go ye into all the world, and preach the gospel to every creature.

Matthew 4:19

And he saith unto them, Follow me, and I will make you fishers of men.

Acts 5:42

And daily in the temple, and in every house, they ceased not to teach and preach Jesus Christ.

John 12:32

And I, if I be lifted up from the earth, will draw all men unto me.

Daniel 12:3

And they that be wise shall shine as the brightness of the firmament; and they that turn many to righteousness as the stars for ever and ever.

Proverbs 11:30

Sister Kadee

The fruit of the righteous is a tree of life; and he that winneth souls is wise.

Ecclesiastes 12:13

Let us hear the conclusion of the whole matter: Fear God, and keep his commandments: for this is the whole duty of man.

Matthew 28:19-20

Go ye therefore, and teach all nations, baptizing them in the name of the Father, and of the Son, and of the Holy Ghost: Teaching them to observe all things whatsoever I have commanded you: and, lo, I am with you alway, even unto the end of the world. Amen.

Matthew 5:14,16

Ye are the light of the world. A city that is set on a hill cannot be hid. Let your light so shine before men, that they may see your good works, and glorify your Father which is in heaven.

2 Timothy 2:2

And the things that thou hast heard of me among many witnesses, the same commit thou to faithful men, who shall be able to teach others also.

Proverbs 14:25

A true witness delivereth souls: but a deceitful witness speaketh lies.

1 Corinthians 2:4-5

And my speech and my preaching was not with enticing words of man's wisdom, but in demonstration of the Spirit and of power: That your faith should not stand in the wisdom of men, but in the power of God.

Luke 9:2

And he sent them to preach the kingdom of God, and to heal the sick.

Ezekiel 3:17-19

Son of man, I have made thee a watchman unto the house of Israel: therefore hear the word at my mouth, and give them warning from me. When I say unto the wicked, Thou shalt surely die; and thou givest him not warning, nor speakest to warn the wicked from his wicked way, to save his life; the same wicked man shall die in his iniquity; but his blood will I require at thine hand. Yet if thou warn the wicked, and he turn not from his wickedness, nor from his wicked way, he shall die in his iniquity; but thou hast delivered thy soul.

1 Corinthians 9:16

For though I preach the gospel, I have nothing to glory of: for necessity is laid upon me; yea, woe is unto me, if I preach not the gospel!

John 6:27

Labour not for the meat which perisheth, but for that meat which endureth unto everlasting life, which the Son of man shall give unto you: for him hath God the Father sealed.

Romans 12:11

Not slothful in business; fervent in spirit; serving the Lord.

Commentary

● The greatest work in the world is to witness the Words of God, to preach the Gospel, to tell people about God's Love. To show them the Love of Jesus.

● The most important job for anybody right after they get saved and filled with the Spirit is to get out witnessing, sharing their testimony and winning others into the Kingdom of God.

● Witnessing His wonder working Words to the world is our major task. Witnessing is more important than winning. What they do with our witness is up to them, as each must make his own decision.

- Even God can't win them all right now, but He wants to give them all a chance.

- Going is not an option, it is a commandment!

- If you have the Love of Jesus, you cannot hide it! If you have Him in your heart… if you have His Love you'll show it, you'll tell others and you'll share it with them.

- Our job is to try to clean up the World, and the best way to do that is by cleansing people's hearts and minds with the Love of God, the power of Christ and the pure knowledge of His Word.

- If you dont speak out and witness when you should, you're literally denying the Lord by keeping your mouth shut.

- Our job is to witness, to win souls and take care of the results.

- He won't bless any other area in your life if you neglect the number one job you have to do, to preach the Word, and number two, to try to win those to whom you preach it.

- Listening is half the job of being a witness!

- Your job is to tell them the truth and to show them love. Their job is to receive it and believe it.

- Once you've given them the Work, your job is done, and there is no use arguing about it any further.

- No matter how effective a witness you are, the fruits are in the hands of the Lord and the response is up to each individual. You can't force results! It's God who gives the increase (1Corinthians 3:7)

- Our job is not done just when people get saved… it's not done until they are disciples and are witnessing and winning souls themselves!

- Don't ever think because there's so much darkness that it's no use to have such a small light, because even one candle can be seen a mile away when it is dark.

- To love them is to weep with them that weep, to suffer with them that suffer, and to feel the agony of heart with them whose hearts are broken.

- Your love didn't fail us Lord! Help our love not to fail others.

- If you love someone, you love them all the way! All the way to heaven and all the way through eternity.

THE WORD

1 Peter 2:2

As newborn babes, desire the sincere milk of the word, that ye may grow thereby.

John 1:1,14

In the beginning was the Word, and the Word was with God, and the Word was God. And the Word was made flesh, and dwelt among us, (and we beheld his glory, the glory as of the only begotten of the Father,) full of grace and truth.

Matthew 4:4

But he answered and said, It is written, Man shall not live by bread alone, but by every word that proceedeth out of the mouth of God.

Psalms 119:11

Thy word have I hid in mine heart, that I might not sin against thee.

John 15:3

Now ye are clean through the word which I have spoken unto you.

Psalms 119:130

The entrance of thy words giveth light; it giveth understanding unto the simple.

2 Timothy 2:15

Study to shew thyself approved unto God, a workman that needeth not to be ashamed, rightly dividing the word of truth.

Hebrews 4:12

For the word of God is quick, and powerful, and sharper than any twoedged sword, piercing even to the dividing asunder of soul and spirit, and of the joints and marrow, and is a discerner of the thoughts and intents of the heart.

John 6:63

It is the spirit that quickeneth; the flesh profiteth nothing: the words that I speak unto you, they are spirit, and they are life.

Matthew 24:35

Heaven and earth shall pass away, but my words shall not pass away.

Commentary

• The secret of power and victory and overcoming and fruitfulness and fire and life and warmth and health and light and leadership… EVERYTHING is in the Bible.

• The most important thing is to hear the Words of God, because that is what keeps you on the straight and narrow way, in tune with and obedient to God.

• Please don't neglect the Word! Read, study, memorise and enjoy it, for it is food for your soul and gives you strength for the battles.

• The Bible is the most wonderful book in the whole world, which can tell you the answers to everything!

• The Bible is the Standard by which all christians should measure all truth, and all error.

• Someday, what you've implanted in your heart may be the only Word of God you've got!

• The minute you start crowding the Word out of your life, you are getting too busy.

• It's a damnable doctrine of church devils to confine all the truth and revelations of God strictly to the

Bible! True prophecy won't teach anything contrary, but it sure can fill in a lot of gaps with the living Word within us.

• They are better than gold and better than silver, the Words of Love that speak to thee through thy Father.

• With every verse you read you are clearing away the churchy rubble, getting rid of man's debris, and pushing aside the preachers' litter to uncover for you what the Bible REALLY says and means, what Jesus taught, and how He really lived!

LOVE

1 Corinthians 13:13

And now abideth faith, hope, love, these three; but the greatest of these is love.

Matthew 22:37-40

Jesus said unto him, Thou shalt love the Lord thy God with all thy heart, and with all thy soul, and with all thy mind. This is the first and great commandment. And the second is like unto it, Thou shalt love thy neighbour as thyself. On these two commandments hang all the law and the prophets.

John 13:34

A new commandment I give unto you, That ye love one another; as I have loved you, that ye also love one another.

1 Peter 4:8

And above all things have fervent love among yourselves: for love shall cover the multitude of sins.

1 John 4:7-8

Beloved, let us love one another: for love is of God; and every one that loveth is born of God, and knoweth God. He that loveth not knoweth not God; for God is love.

Galatians 5:14

For all the law is fulfilled in one word, even in this; Thou shalt love thy neighbour as thyself.

John 14:15

If ye love me, keep my commandments.

Galatians 6:2

Bear ye one another's burdens, and so fulfil the law of Christ.

Matthew 25:40

And the King shall answer and say unto them, Verily I say unto you, Inasmuch as ye have done it unto one of the least of these my brethren, ye have done it unto me.

Matthew 7:12b

Therefore all things whatsoever ye would that men should do to you, do ye even so to them: for this is the law and the prophets.

Romans 13:8

Owe no man anything, but to love one another: for he that loveth another hath fulfilled the law.

Colossians 3:13-14

Forbearing one another, and forgiving one another, if any man have a quarrel against any: even as Christ forgave you, so also do ye. And above all these things put on charity, which is the bond of perfectness.

1 Corinthians 13:4-8a

Love suffereth long, and is kind; love envieth not; love vaunteth not itself, is not puffed up, Doth not behave itself unseemly, seeketh not her own, is not easily provoked, thinketh no evil; Rejoiceth not in iniquity, but rejoiceth in the truth; Beareth all things, believeth all things, hopeth all things, endureth all things. Love never faileth.

1 Corinthians 16:14

Let all your things be done with love.

John 15:13

Greater love hath no man than this, that a man lay down his life for his friends.

1 John 4:19

We love him, because he first loved us.

Romans 8:38-39

For I am persuaded, that neither death, nor life, nor angels, nor principalities, nor powers, nor things present, nor things to come, Nor height, nor depth, nor any other creature, shall be able to separate us from the love of God, which is in Christ Jesus our Lord.

Commentary

• God's Love is the answer to everything: It saves souls, forgives sin, satisfies hearts, purifies minds, redeems bodies, wins friends and makes life worth living.

• In God's Family, our greatest Lover is God and our greatest desire is to serve Him.

• True Love, real Love, God's Love, is all the religion you need.

• Oh, with what everlasting Love Ihave loved thee, and how I have sought thee and searched thee out that thou shouldst find Me".

• God's only law is love! Obey it and you can have total love, life, liberty and happiness in the Lord.

• Love is… believing, trusting, helping, encouraging, confiding, sharing, understanding, feeling, touching, caring, praying and giving.

- Love is asking for forgiveness.

- Love is total humility and total sacrifice.

- The greatest need of man is love, so the greatest service to him is love.

- A little bit of Love goes such a long way!

- If you love your neighbor as yourself, you will put yourself in his place and wonder how you would feel if you were there.

- Love prefers the happiness of others to their own.

- If you sew love you're going to reap love.

- Love wasn't put in your heart to stay, love isn't love till you give it away!

- Love is not blind… it has an extra spiritual eye which sees the good and possibilities that others cannot see.

- Love loves the unlovely and casts a veil over countless sins.

- Love has creative power, because God is Love, and He is the Creator!

- God's Love never fails, it's never lost, and whatever has been done in His Love will not fail.

- Everything must be judged from a standpoint of love.

- As long as whatever you're doing is in Love and not hurting anybody, how can you go wrong?

- You believe in Love as much as you love.

- What is Love? It's just Jesus.

- May we always be known for our love!

- Love is the power and light of God!

- Love knows no hours or days… but is always.

- You can only see love as it is expressed or manifested or put into action, like the effects of the wind. You can't see where it comes from or where it is going but you can see its effects around you.

IT'S ONLY JESUS

Matthew 10:20

For it is not ye that speak, but the Spirit of your Father which speaketh in you.

Philippians 4:13

I can do all things through Christ which strengtheneth me.

Nehemiah 8:10b

For the joy of the Lord is your strength.

2 Corinthians 4:7

But we have this treasure in earthen vessels, that the excellency of the power may be of God, and not of us.

Zechariah 4:6b

Not by might, nor by power, but by my spirit, saith the Lord of hosts.

Jeremiah 17:5

Thus saith the Lord ; Cursed be the man that trusteth in man, and maketh flesh his arm, and whose heart departeth from the Lord .

Psalms 127:1

Except the Lord build the house, they labour in vain that build it: except the Lord keep the city, the watchman waketh but in vain.

Psalms 118:8

It is better to trust in the Lord than to put confidence in man.

Acts 4:13

Now when they saw the boldness of Peter and John, and perceived that they were unlearned and ignorant men, they marvelled; and they took knowledge of them, that they had been with Jesus.

2 Corinthians 12:9a-10b

And he said unto me, My grace is sufficient for thee: for my strength is made perfect in weakness. For when I am weak, then am I strong.

Philippians 2:13

For it is God which worketh in you both to will and to do of his good pleasure.

Commentary

● Only God knows what to do and only God knows what He wants done, and only God can do it.

- He will give you power for the hour, grace for the space and wisdom for the wonder!

- God doesn't expect you to do it. All He expects you to do is obey and He'll do it through you.

- I know you can do it, because I know He can do it through you, as long as you depend on Him and His Holy Spirit and His Word!

- Little is much when God is in it!

- All of God's great spiritual giants were weak men who were made strong by His power.

- All glory be to Jesus! He's the One that does it all! We're merely His yielded instruments, vessels of clay in the hand of the Potter.

- If there's anything good you ever do, do you give Him the glory? Do you say, "Thank You Jesus! Don't thank me, thank the Lord, it's all the Lord".

- Keep remembering it's just the Lord!

- You can of your own self do nothing, but by the Spirit of God you can be a blessing and a help and a savior of others.

Sister Kadee

- Many times when you're weakest in the flesh you are strongest in the Spirit, because you just have to completely throw yourself on the Lord!

- We are nothing, Lord, but Thou art everything.

FAITH

Romans 10:17

So then faith cometh by hearing, and hearing by the word of God.

Proverbs 3:5-6

Trust in the Lord with all thine heart; and lean not unto thine own understanding. In all thy ways acknowledge him, and he shall direct thy paths.

Mark 9:23

Jesus said unto him, If thou canst believe, all things are possible to him that believeth.

2 Corinthians 5:7

For we walk by faith, not by sight.

Luke 1:37

For with God nothing shall be impossible.

Matthew 9:29b

Then touched he their eyes, saying, According to your faith be it unto you.

Sister Kadee

Hebrews 11:1

Now faith is the substance of things hoped for, the evidence of things not seen.

James 1:5-8

If any of you lack wisdom, let him ask of God, that giveth to all men liberally, and upbraideth not; and it shall be given him. But let him ask in faith, nothing wavering. For he that wavereth is like a wave of the sea driven with the wind and tossed. For let not that man think that he shall receive any thing of the Lord. A double minded man is unstable in all his ways.

Hebrews 11:6

But without faith it is impossible to please him: for he that cometh to God must believe that he is, and that he is a rewarder of them that diligently seek him.

James 2:26

For as the body without the spirit is dead, so faith without works is dead also.

Romans 14:23b

And he that doubteth is damned if he eat, because he eateth not of faith: for whatsoever is not of faith is sin.

Titus 1:15a

Unto the pure all things are pure.

Hebrews 10:38

Now the just shall live by faith: but if any man draw back, my soul shall have no pleasure in him.

Job 13:15a

Though he slay me, yet will I trust in him.

Isaiah 30:15b

In quietness and in confidence shall be your strength.

2 Timothy 2:13

If we believe not, yet he abideth faithful: he cannot deny himself.

1 John 5:4

For whatsoever is born of God overcometh the world: and this is the victory that overcometh the world, even our faith.

Sister Kadee

Commentary

• Faith is something that is built by faithful study of God's Word. It grows by hearing the word of God.

• Faith is not nothing! "Faith is the substance of things hoped for." It's knowing God and that God is, and that God is going to take care of you somehow if you obey Him and do His will and His work.

• Trusting is a picture of complete rest, peace and quiet of mind, body and spirit.

• Trying to have faith is a work of the flesh! Accepting faith through His Word is a work of God's grace.

• With faith, believing is seeing! Real faith knows God answers prayer!!

• The Lord loves faith! He loves you because you believe Him, just because He said so. It shows your love and your confidence in Him.

• Faith isn't faith unless it's all you're holding onto.

• Fair weather faith is no faith at all! Real faith endures the battle and the storm, even when you are under attack and sinking! Real faith never quits.

- Discouragement is the Devil's favorite weapon, and the only thing that defeats it is faith!

- We don't know what the Future holds, but we know Who holds the future!

- Faith is not only believing that God can, but that God will, and after prayer, that God has.

- God likes the kind of faith that when there is a choice, a decision, an alternative, the great faith still chooses God's best in spite of the other possibilities.

- Faith is to believe what we do not see, and the reward of faith is to see what we believe.

- Faith praises no matter what happens!

- When you're trusting, you're not heard to fret! When you're fretting, you're not trusting yet!

PRAYER

Matthew 7:7

Ask, and it shall be given you; seek, and ye shall find; knock, and it shall be opened unto you:

John 15:7

If ye abide in me, and my words abide in you, ye shall ask what ye will, and it shall be done unto you.

Jeremiah 33:3

Call unto me, and I will answer thee, and shew thee great and mighty things, which thou knowest not.

Mark 11:24

'Therefore I say unto you, What things soever ye desire, when ye pray, believe that ye receive them, and ye shall have them.

John 14:14

If ye shall ask anything in my name, I will do it.

Jeremiah 29:13

And ye shall seek me, and find me, when ye shall search for me with all your heart.

Isaiah 65:24

And it shall come to pass, that before they call, I will answer; and while they are yet speaking, I will hear.

Matthew 18:18-20

Verily I say unto you, Whatsoever ye shall bind on earth shall be bound in heaven: and whatsoever ye shall loose on earth shall be loosed in heaven. Again I say unto you, That if two of you shall agree on earth as touching any thing that they shall ask, it shall be done for them of my Father which is in heaven. For where two or three are gathered together in my name, there am I in the midst of them.

1 John 5:14-15

And this is the confidence that we have in him, that, if we ask any thing according to his will, he heareth us: And if we know that he hear us, whatsoever we ask, we know that we have the petitions that we desired of him.

1 John 3:22

And whatsoever we ask, we receive of him, because we keep his commandments, and do those things that are pleasing in his sight.

Sister Kadee

1 Thessalonians 5:17

Pray without ceasing.

Psalms 106:15

And he gave them their request; but sent leanness into their soul.

Psalms 66:18-19

If I regard iniquity in my heart, the Lord will not hear me: But verily God hath heard me; he hath attended to the voice of my prayer.

James 4:8a

Draw nigh to God, and he will draw nigh to you.

Hebrews 4:16

Let us therefore come boldly unto the throne of grace, that we may obtain mercy, and find grace to help in time of need.

Romans 8:26

Likewise the Spirit also helpeth our infirmities: for we know not what we should pray for as we ought: but the Spirit itself maketh intercession for us with groanings which cannot be uttered.

Luke 22:31-32

And the Lord said, Simon, Simon, behold, Satan hath desired to have you, that he may sift you as wheat: But I have prayed for thee, that thy faith fail not: and when thou art converted, strengthen thy brethren.

Hebrews 7:25

Wherefore he is able also to save them to the uttermost that come unto God by him, seeing he ever liveth to make intercession for them.

Commentary

- The most important job you have is listening to the King: to stop, look and listen!

- God has made promises in His Word, and when you pray, bring those promises with you to remind Him. It's this positive declaration of your faith and your knowledge of the Word whichpleases God.

- You get what you ask for, and what you have faith for! God takes you exactly at your word!

- Take time to hear from God, and He'll take the time to straighten out the problem.

- The very intensity with which you pray and really mean it or desire it is reflected in the answer.

Sister Kadee

- Never be ashamed to ask for help or prayer when you need it. There is great power in united prayer together!

- It's not how long you pray or how much you pray… it's how much you believe.

- He longs for that sweet communion, that union of heart with hearth!

- You can't do the Master's work without the Master's power, and to get it you must spend time with the Master!

- Desperate prayer that is full of faith is the most powerful weapon we have, and can radically alter any situation or heart.

- God knows your needs, but He likes you to be humble and willing to pray and acknowledge Him, then He answers so you can give Him all the thanks and glory!

- We're to pray in the Name of Jesus, ask in the Name of Jesus, claim victories in the Name of Jesus and rebuke the Enemy in the Name of Jesus!

HEALING

Psalms 34:19

Many are the afflictions of the righteous: but the Lord delivereth him out of them all.

James 5:14-16

Is any sick among you? let him call for the elders of the church; and let them pray over him, anointing him with oil in the name of the Lord: And the prayer of faith shall save the sick, and the Lord shall raise him up; and if he have committed sins, they shall be forgiven him. Confess your faults one to another, and pray one for another, that ye may be healed. The effectual fervent prayer of a righteous man availeth much.

Psalms 107:20

He sent his word, and healed them, and delivered them from their destructions.

2 Kings 20:5b

I have heard thy prayer, I have seen thy tears: behold, I will heal thee.

Jeremiah 30:17a

For I will restore health unto thee, and I will heal thee of thy wounds, saith the Lord; because they called thee an Outcast.

Isaiah 40:29

He giveth power to the faint; and to them that have no might he increaseth strength.

Psalms 103:3

Who forgiveth all thine iniquities; who healeth all thy diseases.

Isaiah 53:5

But he was wounded for our transgressions, he was bruised for our iniquities: the chastisement of our peace was upon him; and with his stripes we are healed.

Exodus 15:26

And said, If thou wilt diligently hearken to the voice of the Lord thy God, and wilt do that which is right in his sight, and wilt give ear to his commandments, and keep all his statutes, I will put none of these diseases upon thee, which I have brought upon the Egyptians: for I am the Lord that healeth thee.

Luke 17:14b

And it came to pass, that, as they went, they were cleansed (healed).

Matthew 10:1

And when he had called unto him his twelve disciples, he gave them power against unclean spirits, to cast them out, and to heal all manner of sickness and all manner of disease.

Hebrews 13:8

Jesus Christ the same yesterday, and to day, and forever.

Malachi 4:2a

But unto you that fear my name shall the Sun of righteousness arise with healing in his wings; and ye shall go forth, and grow up as calves of the stall.

Isaiah 45:11

Thus saith the Lord , the Holy One of Israel, and his Maker, Ask me of things to come concerning my sons, and concerning the work of my hands command ye me.

Acts 9:34a

Jesus Christ maketh thee whole.

Mark 16:17-18

And these signs shall follow them that believe; In my name shall they cast out devils; they shall speak with new tongues; They shall take up serpents; and if they drink any deadly thing, it shall not hurt them; they shall lay hands on the sick, and they shall recover.

Hebrews 12:13

And make straight paths for your feet, lest that which is lame be turned out of the way; but let it rather be healed.

Commentary

• Jesus made us, so He can fix us!

• Healing is a little bit of Heaven, a sample of the resurrection, of everlasting life, of the supernatural bodies we are going to have!

• Expect healing! Expect to be cleansed! Rebuke that infection and that pollution of the Enemy in Jesus Name! He should have NO PART in you!

• If God wants to heal, He doesn't need any help! And if He doesn't want to heal, nothing will help.

• Correct the spiritual problems first as well as the food, sex, cleanliness and other living conditions, then trust God utterly in prayer and obedience and you're bound to get results.

- One of the greatest healing factors is faith, to know that God loves you and cares for you and is going to take care of you no matter what happens.

- Healing is a special blessing, a priceless privilege, which, unlike Salvation, He can take away if you don't keep trusting Him for it and giving Him all the glory.

- If you've been sick and you need healing, take communion by faith, and it's there for you.

- Expect miracles! And in Jesus' name you'll get them!

FREEDOM FROM FEAR

Isaiah 41:10

Fear thou not; for I am with thee: be not dismayed; for I am thy God: I will strengthen thee; yea, I will help thee; yea, I will uphold thee with the right hand of my righteousness.

Isaiah 26:3

Thou wilt keep him in perfect peace, whose mind is stayed on thee: because he trusteth in thee.

2 Timothy 1:7

For God hath not given us the spirit of fear; but of power, and of love, and of a sound mind.

John 14:27

Peace I leave with you, my peace I give unto you: not as the world giveth, give I unto you. Let not your heart be troubled, neither let it be afraid.

Psalms 27:1

The Lord is my light and my salvation; whom shall I fear? the Lord is the strength of my life; of whom shall I be afraid?

Psalms 23:4

Yea, though I walk through the valley of the shadow of death, I will fear no evil: for thou art with me; thy rod and thy staff they comfort me.

1 John 4:18

There is no fear in love; but perfect love casteth out fear: because fear hath torment. He that feareth is not made perfect in love.

Psalms 34:4

I sought the Lord , and he heard me, and delivered me from all my fears.

Mark 5:36b

Be not afraid, only believe.

Jeremiah 1:8

Be not afraid of their faces: for I am with thee to deliver thee, saith the Lord .

Psalms 119:165

Great peace have they which love thy law: and nothing shall offend them.

Sister Kadee

Psalms 56:3-4

What time I am afraid, I will trust in thee. In God I will praise his word, in God I have put my trust; I will not fear what flesh can do unto me.

Deuteronomy 31:6

Be strong and of a good courage, fear not, nor be afraid of them: for the Lord thy God, he it is that doth go with thee; he will not fail thee, nor forsake thee.

Matthew 10:28

And fear not them which kill the body, but are not able to kill the soul: but rather fear him which is able to destroy both soul and body in hell.

Luke 10:19

Behold, I give unto you power to tread on serpents and scorpions, and over all the power of the enemy: and nothing shall by any means hurt you.

Proverbs 29:25

The fear of man bringeth a snare: but whoso putteth his trust in the Lord shall be safe.

Psalms 46:1-2

God is our refuge and strength, a very present help in trouble. Therefore will not we fear, though the earth be removed, and though the mountains be carried into the midst of the sea.

Psalms 91:5-7,10

Thou shalt not be afraid for the terror by night; nor for the arrow that flieth by day; Nor for the pestilence that walketh in darkness; nor for the destruction that wasteth at noonday. A thousand shall fall at thy side, and ten thousand at thy right hand; but it shall not come nigh thee. There shall no evil befall thee, neither shall any plague come nigh thy dwelling.

Commentary

- Just like that bright golden sun, the Lord is able to shine on us and chase all of the shadows away, all of the doubts and fears and lies of the Enemy.

- If you trust God and you have faith, then you don't need to worry. You know your Heavenly Father loves you and He's going to take care of everything!

- Faith is the opposite of fear, and when you have faith you cannot fear!

- If fear displaces faith, then you've got problems. But if you cling to God and the Lord and His word and replace fear with faith, then you've got solutions.

- We don't need to fear the Devil or any or all of his angels! Jesus is with us!

- The Lord's protection is just like a force field around us and the Enemy cannot penetrate it!

- Face your ears in the power of His Spirit on the promises of His Word, and you cannot fail!

- You have to fight fear like you fight the evil and you can't just let him take over!

- The two greatest sources of worry and fear are the past and the future… remorse over the past and fear of the future… God's Word forbids worry about either!

OVERCOMING THE ENEMY

James 4:4

Ye adulterers and adulteresses, know ye not that the friendship of the world is enmity with God? whosoever therefore will be a friend of the world is the enemy of God.

1 John 4:4

Ye are of God, little children, and have overcome them: because greater is he that is in you, than he that is in the world.

Isaiah 59:19b

When the enemy shall come in like a flood, the Spirit of the Lord shall lift up a standard against him.

Ephesians 6:10-12

Put on the whole armour of God, that ye may be able to stand against the wiles of the devil. For we wrestle not against flesh and blood, but against principalities, against powers, against the rulers of the darkness of this world, against spiritual wickedness in high places. Finally, my brethren, be strong in the Lord, and in the power of his might.

1 Timothy 6:12

Fight the good fight of faith, lay hold on eternal life, whereunto thou art also called, and hast professed a good profession before many witnesses.

Ephesians 4:27

Neither give place to the devil.

Matthew 17:21

Howbeit this kind goeth not out but by prayer and fasting.

2 Corinthians 10:4-5

For the weapons of our warfare are not carnal, but mighty through God to the pulling down of strong holds; Casting down imaginations, and every high thing that exalteth itself against the knowledge of God, and bringing into captivity every thought to the obedience of Christ.

1 Peter 5:8-9a

Be sober, be vigilant; because your adversary the devil, as a roaring lion, walketh about, seeking whom he may devour: Whom resist steadfast in the faith.

2 Timothy 4:18

And the Lord shall deliver me from every evil work, and will preserve me unto his heavenly kingdom: to whom be glory for ever and ever. Amen.

1 John 3:8b

For this purpose the Son of God was manifested, that he might destroy the works of the devil.

Colossians 1:13

Who hath delivered us from the power of darkness, and hath translated us into the kingdom of his dear Son.

Commentary

- You have but to utter the name of Jesus to fail all the demons of Hell, Oplexicon and Satan himself!

    - The only way you can get rid of the Devil is to defy him, resist him, rebuke him, refuse to obey him and QUIT FEARING him! Give worship to God!

- Through the Name of Jesus you have power over the Devil, and you can command him what to do and where to go!

- The Devil can't stand the Word, or the Name of Jesus.

- You can't keep the birds from flying over your head, but you don't have to let'm build a nest in your hair.

- The Devil can't win, unless you surrender.

- We might not win every battle, but we are destined to win the war!

- Christians, truly saved Christians cannot be possessed by demons or the Devil as Jesus already possesses them. Christians however can be oppressed in mind, body and spirit with torment, disease and discouragement by the Devil and his imps of Hell.

- "Praise the Lord, and pass the ammunition"

- If you want the darkness to flee, it's as simple as turning on the Light!

- That which enters mind, body and spirit is feeding faith, health and purpose, or feeding fear, disease and discouragement.

TRIALS AND TESTS

Psalms 119:67

Before I was afflicted I went astray: but now have I kept thy word.

Psalms 119:71

It is good for me that I have been afflicted; that I might learn thy statutes.

John 15:2

Every branch in me that beareth not fruit he taketh away: and every branch that beareth fruit, he purgeth it, that it may bring forth more fruit.

1 Corinthians 10:13

There hath no temptation taken you but such as is common to man: but God is faithful, who will not suffer you to be tempted above that ye are able; but will with the temptation also make a way to escape, that ye may be able to bear it.

James 1:2-3

My brethren, count it all joy when ye fall into divers temptations; Knowing this, that the trying of your faith worketh patience.

Hebrews 5:8

Though he were a Son, yet learned he obedience by the things which he suffered.

Isaiah 43:1b-2

Fear not: for I have redeemed thee, I have called thee by thy name; thou art mine. When thou passest through the waters, I will be with thee; and through the rivers, they shall not overflow thee: when thou walkest through the fire, thou shalt not be burned; neither shall the flame kindle upon thee.

Hebrews 12:1-2a

Wherefore seeing we also are compassed about with so great a cloud of witnesses, let us lay aside every weight, and the sin which doth so easily beset us, and let us run with patience the race that is set before us, Looking unto Jesus the author and finisher of our faith.

1 Peter 1:7

That the trial of your faith, being much more precious than of gold that perisheth, though it be tried with fire, might be found unto praise and honour and glory at the appearing of Jesus Christ.

1 Peter 4:12-13

Beloved, think it not strange concerning the fiery trial which is to try you, as though some strange thing happened unto you: But rejoice, inasmuch as ye are partakers of Christ's sufferings; that, when his glory shall be revealed, ye may be glad also with exceeding joy.

Romans 8:18

For I reckon that the sufferings of this present time are not worthy to be compared with the glory which shall be revealed in us.

James 1:12

Blessed is the man that endureth temptation: for when he is tried, he shall receive the crown of life, which the Lord hath promised to them that love him.

Proverbs 28:13

He that covereth his sins shall not prosper: but whoso confesseth and forsaketh them shall have mercy.

2 Corinthians 1:4

Who comforteth us in all our tribulation, that we may be able to comfort them which are in any trouble, by the comfort wherewith we ourselves are comforted of God.

Sister Kadee

Commentary

- God and His service are not all sorrow and tragedy, but He gives you a few trials and a few testings and a few hard things to go through to bring out the sweetness and best in you.

- It's hard to be bokeh, It makes you want to die! But, then you're willing to live for Jesus!

- God only uses broken men and women.

- Our trials and tribulations and mistakes teach us valuable lessons, and God will work it all out in the end according to His will and for His glory.

- Suffering is good for you: it humbles you and gives you more compassion for others.

- There is no testimony without a test, no triumph without a trial, no victory without a battle.

- The lord lets difficulties happen as a test or a testimony and he an overrule all damaging effects

because you are His child, so that, by His miracle working power, things that seem do not have to be… just like the three Hebrew children in the fiery furnace who came out without even smelling of smoke!

- God gets some of His greatest victories out of seeming defeats!

- The Lord's putting us all through testings, trials and tribulations here to find out just how much we can take, what we are worthy of and what we can handle.

- "For thou shalt suffer many things, many trials, many tribulations and many tests before that day, but I will bring thee forth as pure gold if thy faith fails not!"

CHASTENING

Hebrews 12:6,11

For whom the Lord loveth he chasteneth, and scourgeth every son whom he receiveth. Now no chastening for the present seemeth to be joyous, but grievous: nevertheless afterward it yieldeth the peaceable fruit of righteousness unto them which are exercised thereby.

Job 5:17-18

Behold, happy is the man whom God correcteth: therefore despise not thou the chastening of the Almighty: For he maketh sore, and bindeth up: he woundeth, and his hands make whole.

Ecclesiastes 8:11

Because sentence against an evil work is not executed speedily, therefore the heart of the sons of men is fully set in them to do evil.

Proverbs 15:32

He that refuseth instruction despiseth his own soul: but he that heareth reproof getteth understanding.

Proverbs 27:5

Open rebuke is better than secret love.

Proverbs 22:15

Foolishness is bound in the heart of a child; but the rod of correction shall drive it far from him.

Proverbs 16:6

By mercy and truth iniquity is purged: and by the fear of the Lord men depart from evil.

Commentary

• God's spankings are sometimes hard to take, but they are a token of His love, His "intolerable compliment", and are good for you if you learn your lesson by it!

• Beauty for ashes: A flower is crushed to release its fragrance, a honeycomb smashed to get out the honey, the pressure in the deep dark earth creates a diamond and the trying of the soul that it may shine His Light is more precious than these!

• As the dross is removed from precious metals by fire, so are the impurities of your soul removed. The fire is usually turned down when you feel like you just can't take anymore! You're more precious.

PERSECUTION

2 Timothy 3:12

Yea, and all that will live godly in Christ Jesus shall suffer persecution.

Matthew 5:10-12

Blessed are they which are persecuted for righteousness' sake: for theirs is the kingdom of heaven. Blessed are ye, when men shall revile you, and persecute you, and shall say all manner of evil against you falsely, for my sake. Rejoice, and be exceeding glad: for great is your reward in heaven: for so persecuted they the prophets which were before you.

John 15:20a

Remember the word that I said unto you, The servant is not greater than his lord. If they have persecuted me, they will also persecute you.

Philippians 1:29

For unto you it is given in the behalf of Christ, not only to believe on him, but also to suffer for his sake.

Romans 8:31b

If God be for us, who can be against us?

Luke 21:15

For I will give you a mouth and wisdom, which all your adversaries shall not be able to gainsay nor resist.

Matthew 10:23a

But when they persecute you in this city, flee ye into another.

Matthew 5:44

But I say unto you, Love your enemies, bless them that curse you, do good to them that hate you, and pray for them which despitefully use you, and persecute you.

Luke 21:17-19

And ye shall be hated of all men for my name's sake. But there shall not an hair of your head perish. In your patience possess ye your souls.

John 16:2

They shall put you out of the synagogues(churches): yea, the time cometh, that whosoever killeth you will think that he doeth God service.

Sister Kadee

Acts 5:38-39

And now I say unto you, Refrain from these men, and let them alone: for if this counsel or this work be of men, it will come to nought: But if it be of God, ye cannot overthrow it; lest haply ye be found even to fight against God.

Commentary

- If you do it the right way, the Devil will fight you!

- Persecution is one of the surest signs that your work is finished in an area.

- Being a real Christian is dangerous!

- It's better to be a mover than a martyr.

- God allows persecution for our purification… it divides the faithful from the fearful.

- Persecution makes the weak weaker, but the strong stronger!

- When they touch you and attack you, the Lord's anointed, His warriors, they are poking God in the eye!

- God's pattern for His people is the same throughout all history… Witnessing, harvesting souls, persecution, flight, God's wrath.

THANKFULNESS & COMPLAINING

1 Corinthians 10:10

Neither murmur ye, as some of them also murmured, and were destroyed of the destroyer.

1 Thessalonians 5:16-18

Rejoice evermore. Pray without ceasing. In every thing give thanks: for this is the will of God in Christ Jesus concerning you.

Philippians 2:14

Do all things without murmurings and disputings.

Ephesians 5:20

Giving thanks always for all things unto God and the Father in the name of our Lord Jesus Christ.

Romans 9:20

Nay but, O man, who art thou that repliest against God? Shall the thing formed say to him that formed it, Why hast thou made me thus?

Philippians 4:8

Finally, brethren, whatsoever things are true, whatsoever things are honest, whatsoever things are just, whatsoever things are pure, whatsoever things are lovely, whatsoever things are of good report; if there be any virtue, and if there be any praise, think on these things.

Romans 8:28

And we know that all things work together for good to them that love God, to them who are the called according to his purpose.

Commentary

- Doubt, fear, discouragement, murmuring and complaining kill! But faith, trust, courage and praising the Lord maketh alive.

- Complaining is the voice of the Enemy and his doubts!

- God hates complaining! Thank God for your blessings! Thank God for your family, for Love, for Salvation, for protection, for provision, for everything!

- Let's carry the burden of our responsibilities bravely, courageously, cheerfully and thankfully and not be heard to grumble, groan and gripe!

- When things look darkest, don't look down! LOOK UP! Don't murmur and complain… PRAISE THE LORD, HALLELUJAH!

- We have got so much to be thankful for.

- That which you allow to enter the Mind, Body or Spirit is creating a blessed life, or suffering and death.

FAITHFULNESS & OBEDIENCE

Revelation 2:10b

Be thou faithful unto death, and I will give thee a crown of life.

Luke 16:10

He that is faithful in that which is least is faithful also in much: and he that is unjust in the least is unjust also in much.

Matthew 25:23

Well done, good and faithful servant; thou hast been faithful over a few things, I will make thee ruler over many things: enter thou into the joy of thy lord.

1 Corinthians 4:2

Moreover it is required in stewards, that a man be found faithful.

Galatians 6:9

And let us not be weary in well doing: for in due season we shall reap, if we faint not.

John 13:17

If ye know these things, happy are ye if ye do them.

Isaiah 1:19-20a

If ye be willing and obedient, ye shall eat the good of the land: But if ye refuse and rebel, ye shall be devoured with the sword.

1 Samuel 15:22b-23a

Behold, to obey is better than sacrifice, and to hearken than the fat of rams. For rebellion is as the sin of witchcraft, and stubbornness is as iniquity and idolatry.

James 1:22

But be ye doers of the word, and not hearers only, deceiving your own selves.

James 4:17

Therefore to him that knoweth to do good, and doeth it not, to him it is sin.

Commentary

- Faithful people are people who are full of faith.

- To be "found faithful" means loyal, believing and obedient.

- A little thing is a little thing, but faithfulness in little things is a great thing.

- If you're willing to do a little job faithfully, well and diligently, then you're big in God's sight, and He is able to trust you with more!

- God judges us by how we do the little things, because then He knows how we'll do the big things.

- Jesus didn't say, "well done thou good and successful servant", but He said, "well done thou good and faithful servant", He doesn't judge you by how successful you are, but by how faithful you are!

- Your happiness, your health and your blessings depend on your obedience to God.

- Nothing short of right is right!

- How can God bless disobedience?

- Those who love Him most, follow Him closest.

- As we begin to obey and continue to obey, God will supply all the necessary needs… and MORE… and will bless us beyond measure for our faithfulness.

- If you know you're doing your best to please and obey Him, God will do almost anything for you, some of the most amazing things you could possibly imagine!

- God never fails IF we obey.

YIELDEDNESS

John 3:30

He must increase, but I must decrease.

Romans 12:1

I beseech you therefore, brethren, by the mercies of God, that ye present your bodies a living sacrifice, holy, acceptable unto God, which is your reasonable service.

Luke 22:42

Saying, Father, if thou be willing, remove this cup from me: nevertheless not my will, but thine, be done.

Romans 6:13

Neither yield ye your members as instruments of unrighteousness unto sin: but yield yourselves unto God, as those that are alive from the dead, and your members as instruments of righteousness unto God.

Matthew 6:9-13

After this manner therefore pray ye: Our Father which art in heaven, Hallowed be thy name. Thy kingdom come. Thy will be done in earth, as it is in heaven. Give us this day our daily bread. And forgive us our debts, as we forgive our debtors. And lead us not into temptation, but deliver us from evil: For thine is the kingdom, and the power, and the glory, for ever. Amen.

Ephesians 3:20-21a

Now unto him that is able to do exceeding abundantly above all that we ask or think, according to the power that worketh in us, Unto him be glory.

2 Timothy 1:12b

I am not ashamed: for I know whom I have believed, and am persuaded that he is able to keep that which I have committed unto him against that day.

Proverbs 14:26

In the fear of the Lord is strong confidence: and his children shall have a place of refuge.

Commentary

- Your happiness, your health and your blessings depend on your obedience to God.

- Nothing short of right is right!

- How can God bless disobedience?

- Those who love Him most, follow Him closest.

- As we begin to obey, and continue to obey, God will supply all the necessary needs… and more… and will bless us beyond measure for our faithfulness.

- If you know you're doing your best to please and obey Him, God will do almost anything for you, some of the most amazing things you could possibly imagine!

- He never fails if we obey!

- How to find the will of God? Utter abandonment to God… utter yieldedness of the mind, of the body, of your own will, then you will know!

- If you're willing to be what God wants you to be, not what you are but what God wants you to be, then He can mightily use you!

- Let go and let God!

- Ready to go, ready to stay, ready for my place to fill… Ready for service, lowly or great, ready to do His will!

LEADERS

1 Corinthians 11:1

Be ye followers of me, even as I also am of Christ.

Philippians 4:9

Those things, which ye have both learned, and received, and heard, and seen in me, do: and the God of peace shall be with you.

Hebrews 13:17

Obey them that have the rule over you, and submit yourselves: for they watch for your souls, as they that must give account, that they may do it with joy, and not with grief: for that is unprofitable for you.

Matthew 23:11

But he that is greatest among you shall be your servant.

John 10:11b

The good shepherd giveth his life for the sheep.

Proverbs 27:23

Be thou diligent to know the state of thy flocks, and look well to thy herds.

1 Timothy 5:17

Let the elders that rule well be counted worthy of double honour, especially they who labour in the word and doctrine.

1 Peter 5:5-7

Likewise, ye younger, submit yourselves unto the elder. Yea, all of you be subject one to another, and be clothed with humility: for God resisteth the proud, and giveth grace to the humble. Humble yourselves therefore under the mighty hand of God, that he may exalt you in due time: Casting all your care upon him; for he careth for you.

Proverbs 11:14

Where no counsel is, the people fall: but in the multitude of counselors there is safety.

Commentary

- The main job of a shepherd is to keep in touch with the Lord.

- Complete dependence on the Lord is the secret of good leadership… LET GOD LEAD.

- You'd better get busy and take care of your sheep, feed them, protect them, provide for them, care for them, love them and keep them in fellowship with each other, or you are failing in your task as a shepherd.

• Leaders must have a tremendous knowledge of the Word and be able to give the Word. That's the ministry of shepherds: to feed the sheep.

• You'll never be a truly great shepherd until you learn to have compassion on the sheep… until you learn to have great love and great mercy.

• Others may, you cannot! You have to lift up the standard and try to bring others up to what the ought to be and not let yourself get dragged down by them.

• The boss may not always be right, but he is still the boss.

• These four unseen gifts are the most important gifts that any leader can have: knowledge, wisdom, discernment and faith.

• A leader is a servant of the follower! You are our servant Lord, waiting upon us all, ministering rather than being ministered unto! You are the greatest sample of all! The greatest of all samples of humility, mercy and love.

FRUITFULNESS

John 15:4-5

Abide in me, and I in you. As the branch cannot bear fruit of itself, except it abide in the vine; no more can ye, except ye abide in me. I am the vine, ye are the branches: He that abideth in me, and I in him, the same bringeth forth much fruit: for without me ye can do nothing.

Matthew 7:18-20

A good tree cannot bring forth evil fruit, neither can a corrupt tree bring forth good fruit. Every tree that bringeth not forth good fruit is hewn down, and cast into the fire. Wherefore by their fruits ye shall know them.

Psalms 1:3

And he shall be like a tree planted by the rivers of water, that bringeth forth his fruit in his season; his leaf also shall not wither; and whatsoever he doeth shall prosper.

John 12:24

Verily, verily, I say unto you, Except a corn of wheat fall into the ground and die, it abideth alone: but if it die, it bringeth forth much fruit.

Commentary

- We must not only win souls, but we must make disciples of those souls, or we are going to become a fruitless, dying church.

- Good works will produce good fruit.

- The true test as to whether a disciple is actually fruitful or not is not just going on a mission trip, gaining new members to a congregation, helping the poor or even how many people you witness to. Fruitfulness is winning souls, then creating disciples who are able to win souls in the mission field of the world… starting in your own backyard.

GIVING

Matthew 10:8

Heal the sick, cleanse the lepers, raise the dead, cast out devils: freely ye have received, freely give.

Proverbs 3:27

Withhold not good from them to whom it is due, when it is in the power of thine hand to do it.

Luke 6:38

Give, and it shall be given unto you; good measure, pressed down, and shaken together, and running over, shall men give into your bosom. For with the same measure that ye mete withal it shall be measured to you again.

James 2:15-17

If a brother or sister be naked, and destitute of daily food, And one of you say unto them, Depart in peace, be ye warmed and filled; notwithstanding ye give them not those things which are needful to the body; what doth it profit? Even so faith, if it hath not works, is dead, being alone.

2 Corinthians 9:6-7

But this I say, He which soweth sparingly shall reap also sparingly; and he which soweth bountifully shall reap also bountifully. Every man according as he purposeth in his heart, so let him give; not grudgingly, or of necessity: for God loveth a cheerful giver.

Matthew 5:42

Give to him that asketh thee, and from him that would borrow of thee turn not thou away.

Commentary

- You never lose by giving! You can't outgive God.

- The richest people in the World in God's Kingdom are going to be those who share the most.

- If Christianity does not reach down into your pocket, if the Love of Jesus doesn't causes you to share what you have with those in need, then it is false Christianity.

- God will judge you according to not just how much you give or tithe, but by what you have left and your motive in giving. If your reward is a tax write off, you have received your reward.

- If you don't give an offering, God will take a collection!

- When we don't give willingly or cheerfully, then we are not really giving.

- As you pour out, He'll pour in, and you can never outpour Him!

- You can even cast in ALL YOUR LIVING and still not hurt, because God will bless you for it.

- If you tithe faithfully in faith and obedience because of faith in God's Word, He will take care of you no matter what, and more than reward you for it.

- If you can't GO, then GIVE. If you can't be a disciple, support one!

- God's way to plenty is to give it away!

- You are no fool to give a life you cannot keep for a love you will never lose.

SUPPLY

Philippians 4:19

But my God shall supply all your need according to his riches in glory by Christ Jesus.

Matthew 6:33

But seek ye first the kingdom of God, and his righteousness; and all these things shall be added unto you.

Psalms 37:4-5

Delight thyself also in the Lord ; and he shall give thee the desires of thine heart. Commit thy way unto the Lord ; trust also in him; and he shall bring it to pass.

Psalms 84:11

For the Lord God is a sun and shield: the Lord will give grace and glory: no good thing will he withhold from them that walk uprightly.

James 4:2b-3

Ye have not, because ye ask not. Ye ask, and receive not, because ye ask amiss, that ye may consume it upon your lusts.

Romans 8:32

He that spared not his own Son, but delivered him up for us all, how shall he not with him also freely give us all things?

1 Corinthians 9:14

Even so hath the Lord ordained that they which preach the gospel should live of the gospel.

Malachi 3:10

Bring ye all the tithes into the storehouse, that there may be meat in mine house, and prove me now herewith, saith the Lord of hosts, if I will not open you the windows of heaven, and pour you out a blessing, that there shall not be room enough to receive it.

Psalms 34:9-10

O fear the Lord , ye his saints: for there is no want to them that fear him. The young lions do lack, and suffer hunger: but they that seek the Lord shall not want any good thing.

Psalms 37:25

I have been young, and now am old; yet have I not seen the righteous forsaken, nor his seed begging bread.

Commentary

• Keep serving Jesus and He'll serve you well!

• He abundantly heaps more than our needs upon us, as long as we are faithful to serve Him and do His will and preach His Gospel and faithfully witness to others.

• If God fails to take care of His Own, He is worse than an infidel! (1Timothy 5:8)

• There's just no excuse for any servant of God not to have enough support. If you're pleasing God and doing the right thing, He will drop it out of the sky if He has to!

• Our God is a God of miracles and He can supply it from some of the most unexpected sources and through what seem to be the most inopportune occasions.

• Where God guides, He provides!

• If you seek, knock and ask He'll help you find, open and get!

• He's more willing to give than we are to receive.

• God has unlimited capacity to give, and what you get is only limited by your own capacity to receive.

- Be wise in your giving as many false prophets, pastors and teachers are servants of money in disguise. God would rather you give to a homeless man than a megachurch!

END OF THE WORLD

Luke 9:2

But I tell you of a truth, there be some standing here, which shall not taste of death, till they see the kingdom of God.

Luke 11:50-51

That the blood of all the prophets, which was shed from the foundation of the world, may be required of this generation; from the blood of Abel unto the blood of Zacharias, which perished between the altar and the temple: verily I say unto you, It shall be required of this generation.

Luke 18:31

Then he took unto him the twelve, and said unto them, Behold, we go up to Jerusalem, and all things that are written by the prophets concerning the Son of man shall be accomplished.

Matthew 23:36

Verily I say unto you, All these things shall come upon this generation.

Matthew 24:1-2

And Jesus went out, and departed from the temple: and his disciples came to him for to shew him the buildings of the temple. And Jesus said unto them, See ye not all these things? verily I say unto you, There shall not be left here one stone upon another, that shall not be thrown down.

Matthew 24:34

Verily I say unto you, This generation shall not pass, till all these things be fulfilled.

Matthew 26:64

Jesus saith unto him, Thou hast said: nevertheless I say unto you, Hereafter shall ye see the Son of man sitting on the right hand of power, and coming in the clouds of heaven.

Matthew 27:50-53,55

And many women were there beholding afar off, which followed Jesus from Galilee, ministering unto him: Jesus, when he had cried again with a loud voice, yielded up the ghost. And, behold, the veil of the temple was rent in twain from the top to the bottom; and the earth did quake, and the rocks rent; and the graves were opened; and many bodies of the saints which slept arose, and came out of the graves. after his resurrection, and went into the holy city, and appeared unto many.

Mark 8:38

Whosoever therefore shall be ashamed of me and of my words in this adulterous and sinful generation; of him also shall the Son of man be ashamed, when he cometh in the glory of his Father with the holy angels.

Mark 9:1

And he said unto them, Verily I say unto you, That there be some of them that stand here, which shall not taste of death, till they have seen the kingdom of God come with power.

Mark 14:62

And Jesus said, I am: and ye shall see the Son of man sitting on the right hand of power, and coming in the clouds of heaven.

John 12:31

Now is the judgment of this world: now shall the prince of this world be cast out.

Matthew 24:14

And this gospel of the kingdom shall be preached in all the world for a witness unto all nations; and then shall the end come.

Romans 1:8

First, I thank my God through Jesus Christ for you all, that your faith is spoken of throughout the whole world.

Romans 10:18

But I say, Have they not heard? Yes verily, Their sound went into all the earth, And their words unto the ends of the world.

Romans 13:11-12

And that, knowing the time, that now it is high time to awake out of sleep: for now is our salvation nearer than when we believed. The night is far spent, the day is at hand: let us therefore cast off the works of darkness, and let us put on the armour of light.

Hebrews 9:26

For then must he often have suffered since the foundation of the world: but now once in the end of the world hath he appeared to put away sin by the sacrifice of himself.

Hebrews 10:37

For yet a little while, And he that shall come will come, and will not tarry.

Sister Kadee

1 Peter 4:7a

But the end of all things is at hand.

1 John 2:18

Little children, it is the last time: and as ye have heard that antichrist shall come, even now are there many antichrists; whereby we know that it is the last time.

Revelation 1:1a

The Revelation of Jesus Christ, which God gave unto him, to shew unto his servants things which must shortly come to pass.

Revelation 1:3

Blessed is he that readeth, and they that hear the words of this prophecy, and keep those things which are written therein: for the time is at hand.

Revelation 1:7

Behold, he cometh with clouds; and every eye shall see him, and they also which pierced him: and all kindreds of the earth shall wail because of him. Even so, Amen.

Revelation 1:9

I John, who also am your brother, and companion in tribulation, and in the kingdom and patience of Jesus Christ, was in the isle that is called Patmos, for the word of God, and for the testimony of Jesus Christ.

Revelation 5:5

And one of the elders saith unto me, Weep not: behold, the Lion of the tribe of Juda, the Root of David, hath prevailed to open the book, and to loose the seven seals thereof.

Commentary

• When Jesus was speaking to His disciples, telling them that some of them standing there would see Him coming in glory, that He meant 2000 years from then? Jesus is not a liar!

• Jesus clearly said that the generation He was speaking to was the LAST! The last of the old covenant, the old world, and that THAT generation would fulfill all that was pophecied of Him, including the wrath that came upon Jerusalem in 70 AD!

• The Temple in Israel was surely destroyed by Roman Caesars as Jesus said it would be in Mathew 24. Not one stone stood upon another, as the soldiers removed EVERY stone from upon Each other to retrieve all the melted gold.. So then what? PAUSE for 2000 years and MAYBE we will see His day coming and the rest of that prophecy fulfilled.

• The Historical account of Josephus outlines the fulfillment of all timeline prophecies from Daniel, Jesus and Revelations regarding the Great Tribulation, and even Jesus coming in the clouds with glory as well as many other prophecies the blind are waiting for.

• John, in his famous letters to the churches in the book of Revelation, were ACTUAL churches in that day, not some far off imagination of a church, or a metaphor of a church to come 2000 years later!

• ALL was fulfilled in THAT generation, or Jesus, Paul, and John are liars!

• The end of ALL things, must shortly come to pass, this generation, some of you standing here, quickly, all these things spoken were to the people standing with Jesus. NOT US!

• As Jesus died upon the cross many of the prophecies were fulfilled that are still being waited for by the systemite "Christians". The earthquakes, the signs of the Sun and Moon, the graves opened by Jesus, and Satan bound in the bottomless pit.

• Oh, how Satan is using the fear of the end of the world to keep humans as slaves, yet EVERY modern prophet NEVER gets it right… for centuries now! This is another clue the prophecy of Jesus is fulfilled.

- The system of today has Christians so brainwashed, that they believe hollywood movies as scriptural truth, while watching the news in fear of the past prophecies of the antichrist, waiting and praying for a rapture that is not going to happen. Not knowing if they will be left behind. Rapture dysphoria.

- The division among doctrines is damnable to God. The greatest poisoning of the body of Christ in our time coming through the church itself!

DAY OF THE LORD

Revelation 16:16,18,20

And he gathered them together into a place called in the Hebrew tongue Armageddon. And every island fled away, and the mountains were not found. And there were voices, and thunders, and lightnings; and there was a great earthquake, such as was not since men were upon the earth, so mighty an earthquake, and so great.

Revelation 20:2-3

And he laid hold on the dragon, that old serpent, which is the Devil, and Satan, and bound him a thousand years, and cast him into the bottomless pit, and shut him up, and set a seal upon him, that he should deceive the nations no more, till the thousand years should be fulfilled: and after that he must be loosed a little season.

Revelation 20:6

Blessed and holy is he that hath part in the first resurrection: on such the second death hath no power, but they shall be priests of God and of Christ, and shall reign with him a thousand years.

2 Peter 3:8

But, beloved, be not ignorant of this one thing, that one day is with the Lord as a thousand years, and a thousand years as one day.

2 Peter 3:10

But the day of the Lord will come as a thief in the night; in the which the heavens shall pass away with a great noise, and the elements shall melt with fervent heat, the earth also and the works thatare therein shall be burned up.

Amos 5:18,20

Woe unto you that desire the day of the LORD ! to what end is it for you? The day of the LORD is darkness, and not light. Shall not the day of the LORD be darkness, and not light? even very dark, and no brightness in it?

Zephaniah 1:14

The great day of the LORD is near, it is near, and hasteth greatly, even the voice of the day of the LORD :the mighty man shall cry there bitterly.

Joel 1:15

Alas for the day! for the day of the LORD is at hand, and as a destruction from the Almighty shall it come. 63

Joel 2:11

And the LORD shall utter his voice before his army: for his camp is very great: for he is strong that executeth his word: for the day of the LORD is great and very terrible; and who can abide it?

Zechariah 14:1,3

Behold, the day of the LORD cometh, and thy spoil shall be divided in the midst of thee. Then shall theLORD go forth, and fight against those nations, as when he fought in the day of battle.

2 Corinthians 1:14b

Even as ye also are our's in the day of the Lord Jesus.

Commentary

- The dark ages were the Day of the Lord, as spoken of by the Prophets, 1000 years of famine, plagues and no rain for those nations who did not follow Him and keep His Feast and commandments.

- The Millennial Reign of Jesus and the Saints is often confused with prophecy about the New Heaven and New Earth.

- Many claim Tartarian Structures and even Greco-Roman wireless energy structures to be a part of Jesus' and the Saints Millenial Kingdom… which is absurd. These structures are filled with pagan idols and graven images of lesser gods, and even the Christian themed basillacas and cathedrals go against the commandments of God. (Exodus 20:4,5)

• Preterism is a planted nominal religion, just like all the rest. Their data on fulfillment of prophecy in the 1st century is remarkably sound, until we open our eyes and see we are on an ancient, corrupted and disolving earth compared to before the flood of Noah. This is NOT the New Earth of promise.

• By the mouth of 2-3 witnesses let every word be established. 2 Native Americn Elders from different tribes back in early 2000 provided primary evidence to me that Jesus was here in the United States after the resurrection.

• Sioux Activist and Actor, Floyd "Red Crow" Westerman 1936-2007, at an International Indigenous Treaty Counsel gathering, elbowed me in the ribs as I was standing by the fire pondering my participation in Sweat Lodges and Sunrise Ceremonies as a Christian. He told me, "You know, Jesus was here with my people after He was crucified. He came and He danced with us, ate with us, and prayed with us. He told us we were living in a good way on His earth and to keep it up. Then He ascended back up to the Creator above the clouds. We call Him Grandfather".

• Western Shoshone Medicine Man, Spiritual Leader, Activist and Author, Corbin Harney 1920-2007 was a man of very few words. He escaped the Indian re-education schools at the age of 5 after his hands were broken for speaking his own tongue, and found refuge in the wilderness with the Grandmothers of theTribe who taught him their history. He told me after volunteering at his healing center, PooHaBa in Death Valley for a few years, and doing feild logistics for his activism occupations, "You know, The Fisher King ruled in San Francisco before the gold rush." Who was the greatest Fisher of Men? Jesus Christ Himself.

• If churches cared as much about the Truth as they do their tax status, ALL of us would know Jesus returned in that generation as He said He would.

SATAN LOOSED

Revelation 20:5a

But the rest of the dead lived not again until the thousand years were finished.

Revelation 20:7-8

And when the thousand years are expired, Satan shall be loosed out of his prison, and shall go out to deceive the nations which are in the four quarters of the earth, Gog and Magog, to gather them together to battle: the number of whom is as the sand of the sea.

Revelation 17:8

The beast that thou sawest was, and is not; and shall ascend out of the bottomless pit, and go into perdition: and they that dwell on the earth shall wonder, whose names were not written in the book of life from the foundation of the world, when they behold the beast that was, and is not, and yet is.

Commentary

- Somewhere in our not so distant past, time has been changed. And not just the monthly calendar from 13 moons (months) but several hundred years added. We are living in the greatest deception of time since time began! We don't even know what day it is!

- The deception in our world today runs so deep that we cannot trust ANYTHING but the Bible.

- You can only believe 50% of what you see, and only 1% of what you hear these days!

- The only Truth available to us lies within the pages of the Holy Bible, which is under attack viciously at every turn.

- Satan himself knows scripture better than most Christians. When he tempted Jesus to become king of the physical world, he used scripture! And how did Jesus defeat the temptations? With scripture!

- Not everyone who crys "Lord Lord" knows the heart of the King.

- Lies are EVERYWHERE! Within our food, medicine, schools, churches, and news. The system belongs to Satan!

- Turn your ear and eye away from every teacher who does not worship Jesus as their King!

- All World Fair Expose from the late 1800's, World Wars, and even minor wars since have been to destroy the evidence of the Millenial Kingdom of Jesus on earth, and other antiquitech to hide free energy, replacing it with oil.

- We are more than conquerors as we walk in His Light!

- The darkest night is just before dawn!

- The time is coming again when true believers of Christ who will not worship the beast will have to live together and share all things in order to survive, just like the first century Christian.

- All of the world's nominal religions and modern nation boundaries were only created in the past few hundred years to control the narrative, rewrite history, and unleash mass deception to get us to war agains God.

- Test EVERYTHING with scripture from the Bible and discernment from the Holy Spirit. Deception is EVERYWHERE!.

- The Book of Mormon was created to control the narrative of Jesus being here in the USA physically after the resurrection, and their Pioneers left a trail of blood behind them.

FINAL JUDGMENT

Revelation 20:11-15

And I saw a great white throne, and him that sat on it, from whose face the earth and the heaven fled away; and there was found no place for them. And I saw the dead, small and great, stand before God; and the books were opened: and another book was opened, which is the book of life: and the dead were judged out of those things which were written in the books, according to their works. And the sea gave up the dead which were in it; and death and hell delivered up the dead which were in them: and they were judged every man according to their works. And death and hell were cast into the lake of fire. This is the second death. And whosoever was not found written in the book of life was cast into the lake

of fire.

Revelation 21:8

But the fearful, and unbelieving, and the abominable, and murderers, and whoremongers, and sorcerers, and idolaters, and all liars, shall have their part in the lake which burneth with fire and brimstone: which is the second death.

Commentary

- You'd better get right with God, receive Jesus before it is too late!

- Only one life will soon be past, only what's done for Christ will last!

- You are born with nothing in your hands, and will leave with nothing in your hands.

- Will your works on earth be counted for a reward from the Father?

- NOTHING in this life is more important than serving God, winning souls, and teaching God's Word!

- What are you doing with your life? For who? Will it last into eternity?

- When the Beast shows up again with peace, safety, and plenty for all will you follow the trail of money, free elctricity and technological gadgets to your demise of being blotted out of the book of life?

- HAVE FAITH! The darkest night is just before the dawn.

NEW HEAVEN & EARTH

Revelation 21:1-2

And I saw a new heaven and a new earth: for the first heaven and the first earth were passed away; and there was no more sea. And I John saw the holy city, new Jerusalem, coming down from God out of heaven, prepared as a bride adorned for her husband.

Revelation 21:4-5a

And God shall wipe away all tears from their eyes; and there shall be no more death, neither sorrow, nor crying, neither shall there be any more pain: for the former things are passed away. And he that sat upon the throne said, Behold, I make all things new.

Revelation 21:7

He that overcometh shall inherit all things; and I will be his God, and he shall be my son.

Revelation 21:22-23

And I saw no temple therein: for the Lord God Almighty and the Lamb are the temple of it. And the city had no need of the sun, neither of the moon, to shine in it: for the glory of God did lighten it, and the Lamb is the light thereof.

Revelation 22:2

In the midst of the street of it, and on either side of the river, was there the tree of life, which bare twelve manner of fruits, and yielded her fruit every month: and the leaves of the tree were for the healing of the nations.

Revelation 22:5

And there shall be no night there; and they need no candle, neither light of the sun; for the Lord God giveth them light: and they shall reign for ever and ever.

Revelation 22:17

And the Spirit and the bride say, Come. And let him that heareth say, Come. And let him that is athirst come. And whosoever will, let him take the water of life freely.

Commentary

- There have been over 2,000 prophecies fulfilled that were spoken hundreds, sometimes thousands of years before they happened, and the final prophecies of the Bible are playing out before our eyes!

- You were born for such a time as this!

Sister Kadee

- Make a way out of the electri-cities, unless you are called there for God's work.

- The safest place to be is in the center of God's will.

- Rejoice! And be exceedingly glad. For Jesus Christ has overcome the world, and is still on the Throne!

FLAT EARTH

Genesis 1:5-6

And God called the light Day, and the darkness he called Night. And the evening and the morning were the first day. And God said, Let there be a firmament in the midst of the waters, and let it divide the waters from the waters.

Genesis 1:14-19

And God said, Let there be lights in the firmament of the heaven to divide the day from the night; and let them be for signs, and for seasons, and for days, and years: and let them be for lights in the firmament of the heaven to give light upon the earth: and it was so. And God set them in the firmament of the heaven to give light upon the earth, And the evening and the morning were the fourth day. And God made two great lights; the greater light to rule the day, and the lesser light to rule the night: he made the stars also and to rule over the day and over the night, and to divide the light from the darkness: and God saw that it was good.

Job 9:6-7

Which commandeth the sun, and it riseth not; And sealeth up the stars. Which shaketh the earth out of her place, And the pillars thereof tremble.

Job 26:7,10

He stretcheth out the north over the empty place, And hangeth the earth upon nothing. He hath compassed the waters with bounds, Until the day and night come to an end.

Job 37:18

Hast thou with him spread out the sky, Which is strong, and as a molten looking glass?

Job 28:24

For he looketh to the ends of the earth, And seeth under the whole heaven.

Habakkuk 3:11a

The sun and moon stood still in their habitation.

Joshua 10:12-13

Then spake Joshua to the LORD in the day when the LORD delivered up the Amorites before the children of Israel, and he said in the sight of Israel, Sun, stand thou still upon Gibeon; And thou, Moon, in the valley of Ajalon. And the sun stood still, and the moon stayed, Until the people had avenged themselves upon their enemies.

Is not this written in the book of Jasher? So the sun stood still in the midst of heaven, and hasted not to go down about a whole day.

Isaiah 45:22

Look unto me, and be ye saved, all the ends of the earth: for I am God, and there is none else.

Ezekiel 1:26

And above the firmament that was over their heads was the likeness of a throne, as the appearance of a sapphire stone: and upon the likeness of the throne was the likeness as the appearance of a man above upon it.

Luke 4:5

And the devil, taking him up into an high mountain, shewed unto him all the kingdoms of the world in a moment of time.

Luke 21:28

And when these things begin to come to pass, then look up, and lift up your heads; for your redemption draweth nigh.

Psalm 104:5

Who laid the foundations of the earth, That it should not be removed for ever.

1 Chronicles 16:30

Fear before him, all the earth: The world also shall be stable, that it be not moved.

1 Samuel 2:8b

For the pillars of the earth are the LORD's, And he hath set the world upon them.

Ecclesiastes 1:5

The sun also ariseth, and the sun goeth down, and hasteth to his place where he arose.

Commentary

- The globe theory was only introduced in the 50's by Nasa which means to deceive in Hebrew.

- ALL civilizations since the beginning of time have depicted earth as flat with a dome until Nasa.

- "Space may be the final frontier, but it was made in a Hollywood basement"! ~Red Hot Chili Peppers.

- What in the universe did the earth rotate around when the sun wasn't even created until day 4!?

- The UN flag is a map of Flat Earth!

- When instructed to "look up for our redemption draws nigh" Lk. 21:28 how would that be possible if half the earth's inhabitants are upside down!?

- Christians who still believe we are spinning through space have fell blindly into the Soul-lure system!

- Outer Space is what the Bible calls outer darkness! Mat. 8:12, 22:13, 25:30

- Aliens are not what "they" tell us! They are fallen angels, demons, hybrid nephilim offspring.

- When Buzz was interviewed by an 8 year old, she asked "why haven't we gone back to the moon?" Buzz replied, "w-w-w-ell, b-b-b-ecause… we didn't go there".

- Who would use a ball for a footstool?! "Heaven is My Throne, and Earth is my footstool". Isa. 66:1, Acts 7:49

- All roads lead to Rome (The Beast) but the straight and narrow road leads to Christ and Life Eternal!

Sister Kadee

- COME ON, LET'S GO!!!!

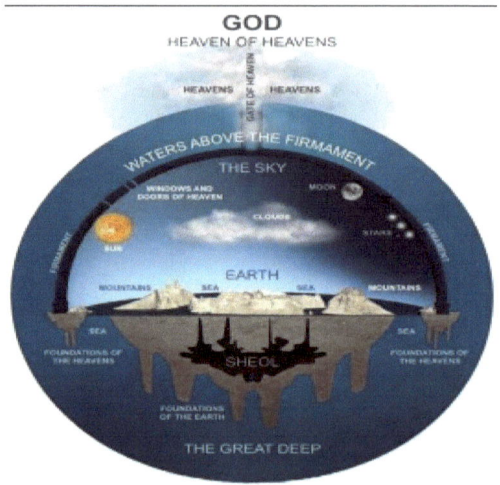

CONCLUSIONS

Let us hear the conclusion of the whole matter: Fear God, and keep his commandments: for this is the whole duty of man. Ecclesiastes 12:13

I am so excited to be a part of your journey as we RISE as the New TEMPLE of God! Welcome to the family and the ever-so-real spiritual battlefield where we war for the souls of mankind as a bright shining light in the midst of gross and evil darkness. The battle is waging strong in this little season of Satan's, where deception and lies are everywhere... even within the church to keep people from knowing who Jesus truly is. We need each other now more than ever dear Brothers and Sisters! We are in this fight to win! We are called to battle and we are more than conquerors... we are God's children, and when we walk with Him we are unstoppable,

no matter how small we are. Use this book to teach others! Start a Home Church or Church in the park! Come! Drink of these Living Waters often! Memorize them! Share them far and wide, for the final judgment is at hand!

I baptize you NOW In the name of the Father, Son, and Holy Spirit! May their Spirit Fire make you into a new creature, full of Love and Life, in Jesus Holy Name.

Sister Kadee

Founder - Pillars Of The Earth Church

"Find the Book @ SisterKadee.com

Learn more about Sister Kadee and her Church

@ Pillarsoftheearthchurch.com

www.ingramcontent.com/pod-product-compliance
Lightning Source LLC
Chambersburg PA
CBHW042325150426
43192CB00004B/115